My Emotion
Journal

Three emotions you've felt today:

1) <u>happy</u>

2) <u>bored</u>

3) <u>anxious</u>

Draw/Stick/Doodle about your day!

You can stick/write, or draw anything in this space!

You could...   Draw your OWN emotion!

Mood Log

How did I feel today in the... (cirlce one!)

Morning?

Afternoon?

Evening?

Is there anything that made you feel frustrated, anxious, angry or sad today? (write or draw!):

I was frustrated and bored in maths. I didn't understand the task. No one helped me.

My friend was off sick, I worried about going to lunch alone.

EXAMPLE PAGE!

 List the top 3 BEST things about today:

1. MY LUNCH! Chocolate brownie!

2. Going ice skating after school.

3. My art class at school.

Three emotions you've felt today:

1) _____

2) _____

3) _____

Draw/Stick/Doodle about your day!

You could...

Draw your OWN emotion!

Mood Log

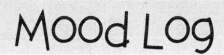

How did I feel today in the... (cirlce one!)

Morning?

Afternoon?

Evening?

Is there anything that made you feel frustrated, anxious, angry or sad today? (write or draw!):

 List the top 3 BEST things about today:

1. _____

2. _____

3. _____

Three emotions you've felt today:

1) _____

2) _____

3) _____

Draw/Stick/Doodle about your day!

You could...   Draw your OWN emotion!

Mood Log

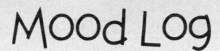

How did I feel today in the... (cirlce one!)

Morning?

Afternoon?

Evening?

Is there anything that made you feel frustrated, anxious, angry or sad today? (write or draw!):

 List the top 3 BEST things about today:

1. _____

2. _____

3. _____

Three emotions you've felt today:

1)_____

2)_____

3)_____

Draw/Stick/Doodle about your day!

You could...  Draw your
OWN emotion!

Mood Log

How did I feel today in the... (cirlce one!)

Morning?

Afternoon?

Evening?

Is there anything that made you feel frustrated, anxious, angry or sad today? (write or draw!):

 List the top 3 BEST things about today:

1. _____

2. _____

3. _____

M T W T F S S   Date: _____

Three emotions you've felt today:

1) _____

2) _____

3) _____

Draw/Stick/Doodle about your day!

You could...   Draw your
                      OWN emotion!

Mood Log

How did I feel today in the... (cirlce one!)

Morning?

Afternoon?

Evening?

IS there anything that made you feel frustrated, anxious, angry or sad today? (write or draw!):

List the top 3 BEST things about today:

1. _____

2. _____

3. _____

Three emotions you've felt today:

1)_____

2)_____

3)_____

Draw/Stick/Doodle about your day!

You could...   Draw your
                      OWN emotion!

Mood Log

How did I feel today in the... (cirlce one!)

Morning?

Afternoon?

Evening?

IS there anything that made you feel frustrated, anxious, angry or sad today? (write or draw!):

 List the top 3 BEST things about today:

1. _____

2. _____

3. _____

Three emotions you've felt today:

1)_____

2)_____

3)_____

Draw/Stick/Doodle about your day!

You could...      Draw your
OWN emotion!

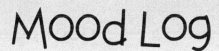

Mood Log

How did I feel today in the... (cirlce one!)

Morning?

Afternoon?

Evening?

IS there anything that made you feel frustrated, anxious, angry or sad today? (write or draw!):

 List the top 3 BEST things about today:

1. _____

2. _____

3. _____

Three emotions you've felt today:

1) _____

2) _____

3) _____

Draw/Stick/Doodle about your day!

You could...   Draw your
OWN emotion!

Mood Log

How did I feel today in the... (cirlce one!)

Morning?

Afternoon?

Evening?

Is there anything that made you feel frustrated, anxious, angry or sad today? (write or draw!):

 List the top 3 BEST things about today:

1. _____

2. _____

3. _____

Three emotions you've felt today:

1) _____

2) _____

3) _____

Draw/Stick/Doodle about your day!

You could...   Draw your
OWN emotion!

Mood Log

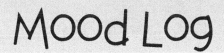

How did I feel today in the... (cirlce one!)

Morning?

Afternoon?

Evening?

Is there anything that made you feel frustrated, anxious, angry or sad today? (write or draw!):

 List the top 3 BEST things about today:

1. _____

2. _____

3. _____

Three emotions you've felt today:

1) _____

2)
_____

3) _____

Draw/Stick/Doodle about your day!

You could...   Draw your
                      OWN emotion!

Mood Log

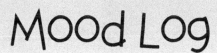

How did I feel today in the... (cirlce one!)

Morning?

Afternoon?

Evening?

IS there anything that made you feel frustrated, anxious, angry or sad today? (write or draw!):

 List the top 3 BEST things about today:

1. _____

2. _____

3. _____

Three emotions you've felt today:

1)_____

2)_____

3)_____

Draw/Stick/Doodle about your day!

You could...   Draw your
                      OWN emotion!

Mood Log

How did I feel today in the... (cirlce one!)

Morning?

Afternoon?

Evening?

Is there anything that made you feel frustrated, anxious, angry or sad today? (write or draw!):

List the top 3 BEST things about today:

1. _____

2. _____

3. _____

M T W T F S S   Date: _____

Three emotions you've felt today:

1) _____

2) _____

3) _____

Draw/Stick/Doodle about your day!

You could...   Draw your
                      OWN emotion!

Mood Log

How did I feel today in the... (cirlce one!)

Morning?

Afternoon?

Evening?

Is there anything that made you feel frustrated, anxious, angry or sad today? (write or draw!):

 List the top 3 BEST things about today:

1. _____

2. _____

3. _____

MTWTFSS Date: _____

Three emotions you've felt today:
1) _____
2) _____
3) _____

Draw/Stick/Doodle about your day!

You could...      Draw your
                                                    OWN emotion!

Mood Log

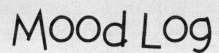

How did I feel today in the... (cirlce one!)

Morning?

Afternoon?

Evening?

Is there anything that made you feel frustrated, anxious, angry or sad today? (write or draw!):

 List the top 3 BEST things about today:

1. _____

2. _____

3. _____

Three emotions you've felt today:

1)_____

2)_____

3)_____

Draw/Stick/Doodle about your day!

You could...   Draw your
                                OWN emotion!

Mood Log

How did I feel today in the... (cirlce one!)

Morning?

Afternoon?

Evening?

Is there anything that made you feel frustrated, anxious, angry or sad today? (write or draw!):

List the top 3 BEST things about today:

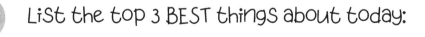

1. _____

2. _____

3. _____

Three emotions you've felt today:

1) _____

2) _____

3) _____

Draw/Stick/Doodle about your day!

You could...   Draw your
OWN emotion!

Mood Log

How did I feel today in the... (cirlce one!)

Morning?

Afternoon?

Evening?

Is there anything that made you feel frustrated, anxious, angry or sad today? (write or draw!):

List the top 3 BEST things about today:

1. _____

2. _____

3. _____

Three emotions you've felt today:

1) _____

2) _____

3) _____

Draw/Stick/Doodle about your day!

You could...   Draw your
OWN emotion!

Mood Log

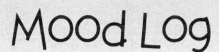

How did I feel today in the... (cirlce one!)

Morning?

Afternoon?

Evening?

Is there anything that made you feel frustrated, anxious, angry or sad today? (write or draw!):

 List the top 3 BEST things about today:

1. _____

2. _____

3. _____

Three emotions you've felt today:

1) _____

2) _____

3) _____

Draw/Stick/Doodle about your day!

You could...   Draw your
                      OWN emotion!

Mood Log

How did I feel today in the... (cirlce one!)

Morning?

Afternoon?

Evening?

Is there anything that made you feel frustrated, anxious, angry or sad today? (write or draw!):

List the top 3 BEST things about today:

1. _____

2. _____

3. _____

Three emotions you've felt today:

1) _____

2) _____

3) _____

Draw/Stick/Doodle about your day!

You could...

Draw your OWN emotion!

Mood Log

How did I feel today in the... (cirlce one!)

Morning?

Afternoon?

Evening?

Is there anything that made you feel frustrated, anxious, angry or sad today? (write or draw!):

 List the top 3 BEST things about today:

1. _____

2. _____

3. _____

Three emotions you've felt today:

1)_____

2)
_____

3)
_____

Draw/Stick/Doodle about your day!

You could...

Draw your
OWN emotion!

Mood Log

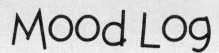

How did I feel today in the... (cirlce one!)

Morning?

Afternoon?

Evening?

Is there anything that made you feel frustrated, anxious, angry or sad today? (write or draw!):

 List the top 3 BEST things about today:

1. _____

2. _____

3. _____

Three emotions you've felt today:

1) _____

2) _____

3) _____

Draw/Stick/Doodle about your day!

You could...   Draw your
                      OWN emotion!

Mood Log

How did I feel today in the... (cirlce one!)

Morning?

Afternoon?

Evening?

S there anything that made you feel frustrated, anxious, angry or sad today? (write or draw!):

List the top 3 BEST things about today:

1. _____

2. _____

3. _____

M T W T F S S   Date: _____

Three emotions you've felt today:

1) _____

2) _____

3) _____

Draw/Stick/Doodle about your day!

You could...   Draw your
                      OWN emotion!

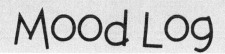

Mood Log

How did I feel today in the... (cirlce one!)

Morning?

Afternoon?

Evening?

IS there anything that made you feel frustrated, anxious, angry or sad today? (write or draw!):

 List the top 3 BEST things about today:

1. _____

2. _____

3. _____

MTWTFSS   Date: _____

Three emotions you've felt today:
1) _____
2) _____
3) _____

Draw/Stick/Doodle about your day!

You could...   Draw your
                                OWN emotion!

Mood Log

How did I feel today in the... (cirlce one!)

Morning?

Afternoon?

Evening?

Is there anything that made you feel frustrated, anxious, angry or sad today? (write or draw!):

 List the top 3 BEST things about today:

1. _____

2. _____

3. _____

M T W T F S S   Date: _____

Three emotions you've felt today:
1) _____
2) _____
3) _____

Draw/Stick/Doodle about your day!

You could...   Draw your
                   OWN emotion!

Mood Log

How did I feel today in the... (cirlce one!)

Morning?

Afternoon?

Evening?

Is there anything that made you feel frustrated, anxious, angry or sad today? (write or draw!):

List the top 3 BEST things about today:

1. _____

2. _____

3. _____

Three emotions you've felt today:

1) _____

2) _____

3) _____

Draw/Stick/Doodle about your day!

You could...   Draw your
                      OWN emotion!

Mood Log

How did I feel today in the... (cirlce one!)

Morning?

Afternoon?

Evening?

IS there anything that made you feel frustrated, anxious, angry or sad today? (write or draw!):

List the top 3 BEST things about today:

1. _____

2. _____

3. _____

Three emotions you've felt today:

1) _____

2) _____

3) _____

Draw/Stick/Doodle about your day!

You could...   Draw your
OWN emotion!

Mood Log

How did I feel today in the... (cirlce one!)

Morning?

Afternoon?

Evening?

Is there anything that made you feel frustrated, anxious, angry or sad today? (write or draw!):

 List the top 3 BEST things about today:

1. _____

2. _____

3. _____

Three emotions you've felt today:

1) _____

2) _____

3) _____

Draw/Stick/Doodle about your day!

You could...   Draw your
                      OWN emotion!

Mood Log

How did I feel today in the... (cirlce one!)

Morning?

Afternoon?

Evening?

Is there anything that made you feel frustrated, anxious, angry or sad today? (write or draw!):

List the top 3 BEST things about today:

1. _____

2. _____

3. _____

M T W T F S S   Date: _____

Three emotions you've felt today:

1) _____

2) _____

3) _____

Draw/Stick/Doodle about your day!

You could...   Draw your
                      OWN emotion!

Mood Log

How did I feel today in the... (cirlce one!)

Morning?

Afternoon?

Evening?

Is there anything that made you feel frustrated, anxious, angry or sad today? (write or draw!):

List the top 3 BEST things about today:

1. _____

2. _____

3. _____

Three emotions you've felt today:

1) _____

2) _____

3) _____

Draw/Stick/Doodle about your day!

You could...   Draw your
OWN emotion!

Mood Log

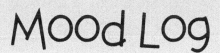

How did I feel today in the... (cirlce one!)

Morning?

Afternoon?

Evening?

Is there anything that made you feel frustrated, anxious, angry or sad today? (write or draw!):

 List the top 3 BEST things about today:

1. _____

2. _____

3. _____

M T W T F S S   Date: _____

Three emotions you've felt today:

1) _____

2) _____

3) _____

Draw/Stick/Doodle about your day!

You could...   Draw your
                                OWN emotion!

Mood Log

How did I feel today in the... (cirlce one!)

Morning?

Afternoon?

Evening?

Is there anything that made you feel frustrated, anxious, angry or sad today? (write or draw!):

List the top 3 BEST things about today:

1. _____

2. _____

3. _____

Three emotions you've felt today:

1) _____

2) _____

3) _____

Draw/Stick/Doodle about your day!

You could...   Draw your
                      OWN emotion!

Mood Log

How did I feel today in the... (cirlce one!)

Morning?

Afternoon?

Evening?

IS there anything that made you feel frustrated, anxious, angry or sad today? (write or draw!):

List the top 3 BEST things about today:

1. _____

2. _____

3. _____

M T W T F S S   Date: _____

Three emotions you've felt today:

1) _____

2) _____

3) _____

Draw/Stick/Doodle about your day!

You could...   Draw your
OWN emotion!

Mood Log

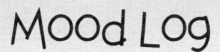

How did I feel today in the... (cirlce one!)

Morning?

Afternoon?

Evening?

IS there anything that made you feel frustrated, anxious, angry or Sad today? (write or draw!):

 List the top 3 BEST things about today:

1. _____

2. _____

3. _____

M T W T F S S   Date: _____

Three emotions you've felt today:
  1)_____
  2)_____
  3)_____

Draw/Stick/Doodle about your day!

You could...   Draw your
                                OWN emotion!

Mood Log

How did I feel today in the... (cirlce one!)

Morning?

Afternoon?

Evening?

Is there anything that made you feel frustrated, anxious, angry or sad today? (write or draw!):

List the top 3 BEST things about today:

1. _____

2. _____

3. _____

Three emotions you've felt today:

1) _____

2) _____

3) _____

Draw/Stick/Doodle about your day!

You could...   Draw your
                      OWN emotion!

Mood Log

How did I feel today in the... (cirlce one!)

Morning?

Afternoon?

Evening?

IS there anything that made you feel frustrated, anxious, angry or sad today? (write or draw!):

List the top 3 BEST things about today:

1. _____

2. _____

3. _____

M T W T F S S   Date: _____

Three emotions you've felt today:

1) _____

2) _____

3) _____

Draw/Stick/Doodle about your day!

You could...   Draw your
OWN emotion!

Mood Log

How did I feel today in the... (cirlce one!)

Morning?

Afternoon?

Evening?

Is there anything that made you feel frustrated, anxious, angry or sad today? (write or draw!):

List the top 3 BEST things about today:

1. _____

2. _____

3. _____

M T W T F S S   Date: _____

Three emotions you've felt today:

1) _____

2) _____

3) _____

Draw/Stick/Doodle about your day!

You could...   Draw your
                      OWN emotion!

Mood Log

How did I feel today in the... (cirlce one!)

Morning?

Afternoon?

Evening?

Is there anything that made you feel frustrated, anxious, angry or sad today? (write or draw!):

List the top 3 BEST things about today:

1. _____

2. _____

3. _____

Three emotions you've felt today:

1) _____

2) _____

3) _____

Draw/Stick/Doodle about your day!

You could...   Draw your
OWN emotion!

Mood Log

How did I feel today in the... (cirlce one!)

Morning?

Afternoon?

Evening?

Is there anything that made you feel frustrated, anxious, angry or sad today? (write or draw!):

List the top 3 BEST things about today:

1. _____

2. _____

3. _____

Three emotions you've felt today:

1)_____

2)_____

3)_____

Draw/Stick/Doodle about your day!

You could...      Draw your
OWN emotion!

Mood Log

How did I feel today in the... (cirlce one!)

Morning?

Afternoon?

Evening?

IS there anything that made you feel frustrated, anxious, angry or Sad today? (write or draw!):

List the top 3 BEST things about today:

1. _____

2. _____

3. _____

Three emotions you've felt today:

1) _____

2) _____

3) _____

Draw/Stick/Doodle about your day!

You could...   Draw your
OWN emotion!

Mood Log

How did I feel today in the... (cirlce one!)

Morning?

Afternoon?

Evening?

Is there anything that made you feel frustrated, anxious, angry or sad today? (write or draw!):

List the top 3 BEST things about today:

1. _____

2. _____

3. _____

Three emotions you've felt today:

1)_____

2)_____

3)_____

Draw/Stick/Doodle about your day!

You could...   Draw your
                    OWN emotion!

Mood Log

How did I feel today in the... (cirlce one!)

Morning?

Afternoon?

Evening?

Is there anything that made you feel frustrated, anxious, angry or sad today? (write or draw!):

List the top 3 BEST things about today:

1. _____

2. _____

3. _____

Three emotions you've felt today:

1) _____

2) _____

3) _____

Draw/Stick/Doodle about your day!

You could...   Draw your
                               OWN emotion!

Mood Log

How did I feel today in the... (cirlce one!)

Morning?

Afternoon?

Evening?

Is there anything that made you feel frustrated, anxious, angry or sad today? (write or draw!):

List the top 3 BEST things about today:

1. _____

2. _____

3. _____

Three emotions you've felt today:

1) _____

2) _____

3) _____

Draw/Stick/Doodle about your day!

You could...   Draw your
                      OWN emotion!

Mood Log

How did I feel today in the... (cirlce one!)

Morning?

fternoon?

vening?

S there anything that made you feel frustrated, anxious, angry or sad today? (write or draw!):

List the top 3 BEST things about today:

1. _____

2. _____

3. _____

MTWTFSS   Date: _____

Three emotions you've felt today:
1)_____
2)_____
3)_____

Draw/Stick/Doodle about your day!

You could...   Draw your
                      OWN emotion!

Mood Log

How did I feel today in the... (cirlce one!)

Morning?

Afternoon?

Evening?

IS there anything that made you feel frustrated, anxious, angry or sad today? (write or draw!):

 List the top 3 BEST things about today:

1. _____

2. _____

3. _____

Three emotions you've felt today:

1) _____

2) _____

3) _____

Draw/Stick/Doodle about your day!

You could...   Draw your
                                OWN emotion!

Mood Log

How did I feel today in the... (cirlce one!)

Morning?

Afternoon?

Evening?

Is there anything that made you feel frustrated, anxious, angry or sad today? (write or draw!):

 List the top 3 BEST things about today:

1. _____

2. _____

3. _____

Three emotions you've felt today:

1) _____

2) _____

3) _____

Draw/Stick/Doodle about your day!

You could...   Draw your
OWN emotion!

Mood Log

How did I feel today in the... (cirlce one!)

Morning?

Afternoon?

Evening?

Is there anything that made you feel frustrated, anxious, angry or Sad today? (write or draw!):

List the top 3 BEST things about today:

1. _____

2. _____

3. _____

Three emotions you've felt today:

1)_____

2)_____

3)_____

Draw/Stick/Doodle about your day!

You could...   Draw your
                      OWN emotion!

Mood Log

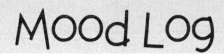

How did I feel today in the... (cirlce one!)

Morning?

Afternoon?

Evening?

Is there anything that made you feel frustrated, anxious, angry or sad today? (write or draw!):

List the top 3 BEST things about today:

1. _____

2. _____

3. _____

Three emotions you've felt today:

1) _____

2) _____

3) _____

Draw/Stick/Doodle about your day!

You could...      Draw your OWN emotion!

Mood Log

How did I feel today in the... (cirlce one!)

Morning?

Afternoon?

Evening?

Is there anything that made you feel frustrated, anxious, angry or sad today? (write or draw!):

List the top 3 BEST things about today:

1. _____

2. _____

3. _____

Three emotions you've felt today:

1) _____

2) _____

3) _____

Draw/Stick/Doodle about your day!

You could...   Draw your
                                OWN emotion!

Mood Log

How did I feel today in the... (cirlce one!)

Morning?

Afternoon?

Evening?

Is there anything that made you feel frustrated, anxious, angry or sad today? (write or draw!):

List the top 3 BEST things about today:

1. _____

2. _____

3. _____

Three emotions you've felt today:

1)_____

2)_____

3)_____

Draw/Stick/Doodle about your day!

You could...   Draw your
                      OWN emotion!

Mood Log

How did I feel today in the... (cirlce one!)

Morning?

Afternoon?

Evening?

Is there anything that made you feel frustrated, anxious, angry or sad today? (write or draw!):

List the top 3 BEST things about today:

1. _____

2. _____

3. _____

Three emotions you've felt today:

1) _____

2) _____

3) _____

Draw/Stick/Doodle about your day!

You could...   Draw your
                                OWN emotion!

Mood Log

How did I feel today in the... (cirlce one!)

Morning?

Afternoon?

Evening?

Is there anything that made you feel frustrated, anxious, angry or sad today? (write or draw!):

 List the top 3 BEST things about today:

1. _____

2. _____

3. _____

Three emotions you've felt today:

1) _____

2) _____

3) _____

Draw/Stick/Doodle about your day!

You could...   Draw your
                      OWN emotion!

Mood Log

How did I feel today in the... (cirlce one!)

Morning?

Afternoon?

Evening?

Is there anything that made you feel frustrated, anxious, angry or sad today? (write or draw!):

List the top 3 BEST things about today:

1. _____

2. _____

3. _____

Three emotions you've felt today:

1)_____

2)_____

3)_____

Draw/Stick/Doodle about your day!

You could...   Draw your
                      OWN emotion!

Mood Log

How did I feel today in the... (cirlce one!)

Morning?

Afternoon?

Evening?

Is there anything that made you feel frustrated, anxious, angry or sad today? (write or draw!):

List the top 3 BEST things about today:

1. _____

2. _____

3. _____

MTWTFSS   Date: _____

Three emotions you've felt today:

1) _____

2) _____

3) _____

Draw/Stick/Doodle about your day!

You could...   Draw your
                      OWN emotion!

Mood Log

How did I feel today in the... (cirlce one!)

Morning?

Afternoon?

Evening?

Is there anything that made you feel frustrated, anxious, angry or sad today? (write or draw!):

 List the top 3 BEST things about today:

1. _____

2. _____

3. _____

M T W T F S S   Date: _____

Three emotions you've felt today:

1) _____

2) _____

3) _____

Draw/Stick/Doodle about your day!

You could...   Draw your
                      OWN emotion!

Mood Log

How did I feel today in the... (cirlce one!)

Morning?

Afternoon?

Evening?

Is there anything that made you feel frustrated, anxious, angry or sad today? (write or draw!):

List the top 3 BEST things about today:

1. _____

2. _____

3. _____

Three emotions you've felt today:

1)_____

2)_____

3)_____

Draw/Stick/Doodle about your day!

You could...   Draw your
                      OWN emotion!

Mood Log

How did I feel today in the... (cirlce one!)

Morning?

Afternoon?

Evening?

Is there anything that made you feel frustrated, anxious, angry or sad today? (write or draw!):

 List the top 3 BEST things about today:

1. _____

2. _____

3. _____

Three emotions you've felt today:

1) _____

2) _____

3) _____

Draw/Stick/Doodle about your day!

You could...      Draw your
                                          OWN emotion!

Mood Log

How did I feel today in the... (cirlce one!)

Morning?

Afternoon?

Evening?

Is there anything that made you feel frustrated, anxious, angry or sad today? (write or draw!):

 List the top 3 BEST things about today:

1. _____

2. _____

3. _____

Three emotions you've felt today:

1)_____

2)_____

3)_____

Draw/Stick/Doodle about your day!

You could...   Draw your
OWN emotion!

Mood Log

How did I feel today in the... (cirlce one!)

Morning?

Afternoon?

Evening?

Is there anything that made you feel frustrated, anxious, angry or sad today? (write or draw!):

List the top 3 BEST things about today:

1. _____

2. _____

3. _____

Three emotions you've felt today:

1) _____

2) _____

3) _____

Draw/Stick/Doodle about your day!

You could...   Draw your
                      OWN emotion!

Mood Log

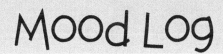

How did I feel today in the... (cirlce one!)

Morning?

Afternoon?

Evening?

IS there anything that made you feel frustrated, anxious, angry or sad today? (write or draw!):

 List the top 3 BEST things about today:

1. _____

2. _____

3. _____

Three emotions you've felt today:

1) _____

2) _____

3) _____

Draw/Stick/Doodle about your day!

You could...   Draw your
OWN emotion!

Mood Log

How did I feel today in the... (cirlce one!)

Morning?

Afternoon?

Evening?

Is there anything that made you feel frustrated, anxious, angry or sad today? (write or draw!):

List the top 3 BEST things about today:

1. _____

2. _____

3. _____

M T W T F S S   Date: _____

Three emotions you've felt today:

1) _____

2) _____

3) _____

Draw/Stick/Doodle about your day!

You could...   Draw your
OWN emotion!

Mood Log

How did I feel today in the... (cirlce one!)

Morning?

Afternoon?

Evening?

Is there anything that made you feel frustrated, anxious, angry or sad today? (write or draw!):

List the top 3 BEST things about today:

1. _____

2. _____

3. _____

M T W T F S S   Date: _____

Three emotions you've felt today:

1) _____

2) _____

3) _____

Draw/Stick/Doodle about your day!

You could...   Draw your
OWN emotion!

Mood Log

How did I feel today in the... (cirlce one!)

Morning?

Afternoon?

Evening?

Is there anything that made you feel frustrated, anxious, angry or sad today? (write or draw!):

List the top 3 BEST things about today:

1. _____

2. _____

3. _____

M T W T F S S   Date: _____

Three emotions you've felt today:
1) _____
2) _____
3) _____

Draw/Stick/Doodle about your day!

You could...   Draw your
                      OWN emotion!

Mood Log

How did I feel today in the... (cirlce one!)

Morning?

Afternoon?

Evening?

IS there anything that made you feel frustrated, anxious, angry or sad today? (write or draw!):

List the top 3 BEST things about today:

1. _____

2. _____

3. _____

Made in the USA
Las Vegas, NV
24 January 2021